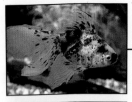

How to Care for Your Goldfish

CONTENTS

Photos by:
Dick Mills
Linda Lewis

KINGDOM

INTRODUCTION

The goldfish is undoubtedly the most popular aquarium fish in the world; so much so that it is more familiar to the average person than any other species, and needs no description. As children, many of us have kept goldfish or at least seen them at friends' houses. In spite of the enormous developments that have taken place in the keeping of tropical fish, the goldfish remains, along with the dog, the cat and the budgerigar, one of the world's most popular pets. The reason for this is not difficult to understand, for the goldfish is an amazingly hardy animal that can stand up to a lot of bad treatment, which is usually the result of ignorance.

I hope that this volume will enable you to gain more enjoyment from your pet, and help it to have a good life in healthy and attractive surroundings.

History

Exactly when the goldfish was first kept in captivity is not known for sure, but it is generally believed that it was during the Chinese Sung dynasty (960-1279 AD). At that time Chi-yu (golden fish) were kept near temples along with the wild types from which they were bred - probably the crucian carp, *Carassius carassius*. From China, goldfish first went to Korea and by 1500 had arrived in Japan, where continued

The Red Comet needs a good-sized aquarium with plenty of swimming space.

selective breeding took place, producing many varieties and colour variations. The first goldfish to reach Europe early in the 16th century probably originated in China.

By the 18th century goldfish were becoming quite popular. Japanese fish first arrived in Europe and America during the 19th century, when at the same time hatcheries in Germany, Italy and elsewhere were being established to cope with the ever-increasing demand for these attractive and tough little fish.

Soon thousands of private individuals, quick to recognise the potential of goldfish, were importing stock from both the Far East and Europe. Today, China, Israel, the USA and Japan are the largest breeders of the many varieties of goldfish that have become established, and the breeding of the more exotic types is now an enormous hobby as well as a profession. China, the original home of the goldfish, still maintains a very strong interest in developing varieties, and breeding stations are run under government control.

This is the Bristol variety of the Shubunkin.

AQUARIUMS

The desire to keep fish in glass tanks, as opposed to outdoor pools, was no doubt greatly encouraged in Europe following the opening, in 1853, of the world's first public vivarium in Regent's Park Zoo, London. Today we apply the term 'vivarium' to the dry or semi-dry tanks used for housing reptiles, but this was not always so. Many thousands of visitors, seeing both freshwater and marine fish alive and swimming about, were soon putting all manner of fish into jars or any other suitable or unsuitable container. Alas, like the zoo-keepers themselves, people found that keeping fish alive for any length of time was not quite as simple as it appeared. However, even today, one still sees fish subjected to the same sort of conditions as they were in Victorian times, and none more so than the poor old goldfish.

Two Golden Orfes.

It is not realistic simply to place your goldfish in a water container, put in a few plants, drop in some fish flakes whenever you remember, and expect your fish to survive well and live a happy life. That some goldfish tolerate such conditions temporarily is not because they are surviving but because they are taking a long time to die. Coldwater fish need as much consideration as tropicals, the main difference being that they do not need heated water. This simple fact believably (and also unbelievably) accounts for the casual way in which they have been treated over the years.

One of the many colour variants now available, a tri-colour goldfish.

A group of Pearlscale and Mixed Fancies living together quite happily.

Goldfish Bowls

In spite of the considerable knowledge of fish needs available today, manufacturers still produce the traditional globular bowls with a narrow neck. Goldfish bowls have nothing to recommend them other than their cheapness. Fish breathe oxygen just as we do, but they extract it from water passed over their gill plates. A goldfish bowl has very little surface area of water and this is what determines the amount of oxygen that a given volume of water contains; therefore it is possible for two similar volumes of water to contain very different amounts of oxygen.

Fish Tanks

The ideal shape of a fish tank is oblong, the length about twice the height; this gives a suitable surface-to-air ratio. The tank can be all glass, plastic (acrylic), or metal-framed glass. The first two are now more popular than the last.

Thousands of beginners start off with the small plastic tanks that come complete with hoods. The drawback is that the tanks tend to scratch easily, and the size restricts the number of fish and plants that they can contain. As a general rule, always purchase the largest tank you can possibly afford, as it will look better, offer more potential for aquascaping, and you can keep more fish in it.

The Oranda combines the long tail of the Veiltail with the hood of the Lionhead.

Filtration

In theory, if there is a good balance between plants and fish, then the water remains in good condition without filtration. In reality, this is rarely the case, so it is better to buy a filter that removes the debris created by the waste from the fish, uneaten food and dead organisms that sink to the bottom of the tank. You get the same result by changing the water in the tank each week, but this is extra work for you and is not actually beneficial to the fish or plants, as they need water that has 'matured' and contains the balance of organisms and minerals which the fish need to maintain good health. Your local aquatic shop will advise you on the type of filter best suited to your aquarium and your family.

Aeration

You can increase the amount of oxygen contained in the water by using an air pump attached to an airstone or similar porous material. Set the airstone near, but not on, the bottom of the tank. Goldfish need more oxygen in the water than do tropical fish, so an air pump is a very useful extra. It has the further advantage that it creates currents that help to keep the temperature at a more constant level throughout the tank. You will not need an aerator if you fit a properly fitted and sized power filter, as power filters have the same effect of disturbing the water surface, so improving aeration.

Light

Set the tank where it will benefit from daylight, but do not put it in direct sunlight. This raises the temperature and reduces the amount of oxygen in the water. It will also increase the amount of algae growing in it, as well as the rate of bacterial growth. Lighting is necessary for healthy plant growth, so fit a suitable fluorescent or tungsten light under the tank canopy. You should also fit a glass sheet on the top of the tank to act as a condensation plate and to reduce surface evaporation of the water. Light will be required for 12 to 14 hours daily.

Temperature

Goldfish will survive within the range of 0-22°C (32-72°F) but the most suitable range is 8-18°C (46-64°F). There are many thermometers to choose from that can be fitted either inside or outside the tank, including those stick-on strips that change colour according to the water temperature. The most reliable types are those that can be immersed in the tank water.

Goldfish kept in home tanks are normally subjected to temperatures near the higher end of their accepted range, and that presents no problem. In fact, many of the fancier varieties of goldfish need warmer temperatures than their more streamlined relatives. Like other aquarium fish, goldfish should not be subjected to abrupt temperature changes.

Above: An uncoloured London Shubunkin.

Below: Where it all started from - the common goldfish.

Water

Although goldfish do not require such specific water conditions as most tropical fish, they do prefer water that is neutral to slightly alkaline. A pH reading of about 7-7.5 will be required. Test the pH with one of the inexpensive kits available from your pet shop or aquatic shop. You can test the hardness of the water with kits as well but, given the hardiness of goldfish and the fact that you will be topping up the tank from your domestic water supply, it is probably just as well that you do not become too fussy about this. If chemicals are added to the tank water at random (and few of us are chemists) then serious consequences may follow: chemicals added incorrectly to the tank can turn a small problem into a big one. Tap water is often chlorinated but you can make it safe either by means of a chemical dechlorinator or by leaving it to stand for two to three days. An air line immersed in it to cause turbulence will speed the process; another good reason for fitting an aerator to your aquarium.

A Black Moor with 'panda' markings.

Gravel

You will need a layer of gravel in your tank to provide a growing medium for the plants and to anchor them firmly in place. This is important, as goldfish enjoy rooting about at the tank bottom in search of food. Goldfish also nibble at plants, but it is worth persevering to establish a good plant growth. The gravel should be of medium to dark colours for best effect, and about 3mm in size. Some people prefer the bright, almost neon-coloured, gravel and this is a matter of personal taste. Before you place the gravel into the tank, put it in a bucket and flush it thoroughly with a hose. Stir up the gravel really hard at intervals throughout this process; when the water runs clear from the bucket, despite the most forceful stirring, the gravel is ready to be placed into the tank.

Rocks

The most suitable rocks for the aquarium are granite, slate and sandstone. Many rocks found in natural water courses can be used, provided that they are free of contaminants and do not have the chemical property to raise or lower the pH of the tank by harmful amounts. Ask at your pet shop if you have any doubts about the suitability of any given rock.

Avoid all rocks with sharp edges and those such as marble, limestone and soft sandstone. These rocks contain a high mineral content that will leach out slowly and make the water far too alkaline for fish and plants. Driftwood, bogwood and African roots are also useful materials for landscaping the aquarium and you can buy these at most pet shops.

Plants

Many plants can be used in the coldwater aquarium, and several of these are also suitable for the garden pond, which may well increase your choice of plants when you are shopping. Select healthy looking specimens, and always wash them thoroughly before introducing them into your tank. Plants not only look nice but provide hiding places for the fish, sites for egg laying and a browsing area, which are important therapeutic aspects often overlooked by those who merely place a few rocks in the tank. A wide variety of plastic plants are sold these days; many are terrible but some are very lifelike and can be used to good effect as background props. I prefer the real plants but have seen artificial ones used extremely effectively.

The term 'aquascaping' is used to describe the overall decoration of the

Compare this London Shubunkin with the one on page 10; the colours are completely different.

AQUASCAPING

aquarium. An aquarium can be arranged in a vast number of ways, varying from very formal, sparsely-planted scenes, through well-planted, well-stocked views, to the more bizarre form of themed aquascaping where a topic is selected and the tank furnished accordingly: sunken cities, galleons, fairyland and so on. Some purists frown on themed aquascaping on the grounds that the scenes are unnatural, but it must be remembered that the goldfish itself is an unnatural variety of fish. More importantly, children often enjoy these types of scenes and I believe that anything that encourages an interest in fishkeeping is to be applauded.

Setting Up The Aquarium

Having purchased your tank and all the necessary accessories, you can now prepare the aquarium for the goldfish. First, before setting anything in the tank, draw up various plans to see how you think your arrangement will look, giving due consideration to the height of the plants, areas left for free swimming, the best layout for rocks, and so on. Bear in mind that essentially there are two ways you can go: you can either aim for an informal setting in which the contents of the tank are set up randomly (applying common sense, of course) or attempt a formal setting in which the contents are set up in neat rows, with left-right balance keenly in mind. I prefer an informal layout rather than a formal one, as I think that it better represents a natural setting.

Allowing for the weight of the final set-up (water, rocks and gravel) you must set the tank on a solid base. I recommend that you put a thick layer of polystyrene or cork under the tank to even out any minor irregularities in the site surface and make sure that the tank is level and the weight evenly distributed. Avoid placing the tank opposite a door where draughts may cause a change in water temperature. This is not good for plants or fish.

Next, place the gravel and rocks into the tank and arrange them so that there is a slope from the back of the tank to the front; say 2.5cm (1in) in front to 10cm (4in) at the rear. Alternatively, you could build a small terrace wall across part of the tank length, about mid-way back, to raise the level and provide a free-swimming area in the foreground; a piece of driftwood bought from a pet shop could be used to the same effect. You should position the rocks so that they can be seen but do not become the focal point and push them into the gravel so that they look natural.

At this stage, if you are going to use an airstone, hide the airline neatly under the gravel and tuck the airstone behind a rock. Do not hide the airstone too well, however, because it will require frequent cleaning. Remember that airstones easily become clogged.

Adding The Water

When everything looks as you want it, cover the gravel with a sheet of paper, and add the water by pouring it gently onto a concave plate or onto glass held at an angle. The paper will make sure that the gravel is not disturbed too much. Half-fill the aquarium and check that the temperature is correct before planting.

Push the plants securely into the substrate using either one of the special tools available for the purpose or your fingers. Once the plants are set to your satisfaction, add the rest of the water until it is about 5cm (2in) from the top of the tank. If you want, you can disguise the waterline by sticking a strip of black tape lengthwise along the top of the tank. Now you can set the tank hood in place and switch on the electricity to test that everything is working.

It is best to leave the tank running without fish for at least three days so that the water has time to mature. You can then siphon off any debris that may have collected at the top of the tank and remove and replace about half of the water. Then wait another few days just to see that the plants are still healthy and anchored securely before adding the fish.

Adding The Goldfish

The final piece in your aquascene are the goldfish themselves. Ideally, you will have quarantined them in a small holding tank to see that they are healthy and feeding well. If you do not quarantine them, make sure you buy from a reputable source. Float the plastic bag in which they were transported in the tank for about 20 minutes so that the temperature of the water in it becomes the same as that in the tank. During this time you can add some of the tank water to the bag so that the fish have the chance to accustom themselves to the different water qualities. Finally, gently open the bag, allowing the fish to swim off and explore their new home.

Once your new tank has had a chance to settle, you may add the inhabitants.

Young black and gold Koi. These fish need more care than the average goldfish, and you may go on to keep them when you are more experienced.

Maintenance
You should clean your aquarium regularly, about every third week. During cleaning, turn off all the electrical equipment and take the plugs out of the sockets to guard against damage or unnecessary danger. Check all the equipment for wear, service the pumps, and so on. It is advisable always to leave tap water to stand for a few days before you clean the tank, ideally in the same room as the aquarium so that temperatures are the same. Replace no more than up to 50% of the water, as this ensures that enough of the micro-organisms beneficial to the tank are retained.

A well-balanced aquarium will give you much pleasure, and the routine upkeep is probably less than for any other pet.

FEEDING

The goldfish is an omnivorous feeder; in other words it eats both vegetable and animal foods. Goldfish eat at all levels in the water and so are most obliging and easily catered for. The feeding of fish has developed considerably over the years, and today there is no shortage of every possible type of nutrient that your goldfish needs.

Nutritional Requirements

The basic constituents of food are: carbohydrates, which provide energy for muscular activity; fats, which provide insulation and reserves of energy and assist in the absorption of vitamins; and proteins, which provide the raw material for tissue and muscle construction.

Another variation of the common goldfish demonstrates the range of colours and finnage that is available nowadays.

When fat levels have been used up protein can be converted into carbohydrate matter; thus, a starving animal becomes 'skin and bone', as protein is the only foodstuff from which tissue can be constructed and is the last level of energy reserves. Beyond these three major constituents, animals need approximately 22 types of vitamins, as well as varying amounts of minerals. These last two items are needed to help in the various metabolic processes and to build up resistance against disease. I should point out that, in spite of the amount of multi-vitamins and mineral supplements produced today, if your fish are supplied with a balanced diet, these additives will not be needed and may actually be harmful.

A fancy goldfish, Black Oranda.

Excess vitamins and minerals must be excreted by the fish, but some of the material will be laid down in bodily tissue, upsetting normal healthy balances and thus creating problems.

The prime sources of these constituents are vegetable matter, animal products, cereals, and dissolved minerals in the water itself. Vegetable matter is an excellent source of carbohydrates and vitamins. Vegetables also contain varying amounts of protein but are short of certain essential amino acids (from which protein is made), and so livefood is needed. Vegetable protein is not assimilated as readily as animal protein, so it is necessary to supply a varied diet at all times. During the breeding period fish need increased amounts of protein, whereas during the non-breeding period they need food which gives them energy. During the winter period (in ponds) when temperatures fall to 8°C or below, fish need no food at all and live on their fat reserves until the spring, provided that they were fed well during the warmer months.

Feeding Methods

The choice of feeding method for the modern aquarist is varied, as is the food itself, which is available as flakes, tablets, pellets, cubes, fresh, freeze-dried and deep frozen.

Commercial foods are carefully formulated to contain all the necessary constituents and a visit to a good aquatic or pet shop will show the vast range available to you. Flakes are very popular with goldfish keepers because they float for quite some time before slowly sinking, thus giving the fish ample time to feed on

Above: The Lionhead is also known as the 'Ranchu' and is highly prized in Japan.

Below: The fluid-filled sacs under the eyes give the Bubble-eye goldfish its name.

them. Besides branded foods, it is strongly recommended that you feed a varied selection of other nutrients to ensure good colour and healthy growth in your fish.

Vegetables, such as carrots, spinach and peas, can be finely shredded, as can various meats, including poultry and fish. Earthworms, whiteworms, daphnia, cyclops, flies (swatted, not sprayed), woodlice and many other forms of livefood can be collected and purchased from your local supplier and fed to your fish. Tubifex, a small worm found in sewage, is an excellent livefood. Some shops sell it live, but you can buy it either freeze-dried or frozen. The important thing is to experiment across as wide a range of foods as possible and try to avoid becoming predictable in your feeding patterns.

When To Feed

The most common mistake made by people new to goldfish is to over-feed them. Your goldfish should only be given as much food as they can eat in two to three minutes.

Uneaten food simply falls to the bottom of the tank, where it decomposes. This adds potentially harmful waste products to the water, which eventually will become cloudy as it becomes saturated with excess products. Under normal conditions, a small feed three times daily is sufficient. Always check that each fish is feeding.

Holidays

As long as they have been well fed beforehand, goldfish will survive up to a week without food. However, when you go on holiday, it is a good idea to ask someone to check up on your fish every couple of days in case of power cuts or tank leakages. If you rely on a friend to feed them during a longer absence, unless he or she is an experienced fishkeeper it might be worth leaving small amounts of food in packets with strict instructions when to feed - and put less-than-normal quantities in the packets just to be on the safe side. You can also purchase feeding blocks that release food over a two-week period.

To recap on feeding: plenty of variety in small but regular amounts.

VARIETIES

Over many centuries of careful selective breeding of various mutations, the common goldfish (*Carassius auratus*) has produced a great number of varieties. It is estimated that well over 100 forms are now available although, in my opinion, many of these are quite grotesque. I find it difficult to understand how their breeding can

The Black Moor should be black all over. It has telescope eyes which take about two years to develop. You can see the fleshy growths in this picture.

be justified on either aesthetic or practical grounds. However, a number show minor modifications to the normal goldfish we all know so well, and the average person will probably start with these. You should remember that the further a particular species is from its natural form, the more difficult it is to keep it. If you plan to keep goldfish in a garden pond, I would recommend that you restrict yourself to the more 'normal' varieties that do not exhibit unusual finnage or head growths, as such varieties tend to be much more delicate. Apart from this, they are seen at their best in the aquarium.

The Common Goldfish

The archetypal goldfish is of classic fish appearance, with paired pectoral and pelvic (or ventral) fins, which are used for balance, braking, turning and slow-speed browsing movements. The single anal fin is largely for stabilisation purposes; the caudal or tail fin is the main source of propulsion and turning, together with the body movements. The large dorsal fin prevents body roll and is thus a stabilising fin. Along the mid-line of the fish is a lateral line. This is a collection of sensory cells that respond to vibrations in the water. From this basic model all varieties have been developed. The multi-finned varieties, such as the Veiltail, have weaker fin rays so are slower moving than those with more traditional fins such as the common goldfish and Comet.

Colours

Goldfish are available in a wide range of colours, including orange, yellow, silver and black, together with many combinations of these colours that create the appearance of blue, red and even brown.

The controlling factor over this range of colours is the reflective layer of tissue known as iridocytes. When this is present, as in normal fish, then the scales are described as 'metallic'. If the upper layer is missing, the effect is termed 'nacreous', as it gives a mother-of-pearl appearance and a greater range of colours because pigment lower in the body tissue is visible. If the reflective layer is missing altogether, the effect is called 'matt', showing that there is no shine to the scales. It is possible for some reflective tissue to be retained in an otherwise lacking fish, giving a few shiny scales, but these are undesirable from a purist's point of view.

Varieties

As stated earlier in this chapter, there are believed to be over 100 goldfish varieties, many of which are fairly common, and some of which I feel are of dubious merit. Some of the most common varieties, which are more suitable for the beginner, are discussed below.

Comet: This hardy, very streamlined fish was developed in the USA. Its tail is as long as the body and deeply forked. It needs plenty of swimming space. It is often yellow but orange is another popular colour. Metallic reflective group.

A fancy Oranda. The black on the fin may disappear when it is older.

Shubunkin: Two varieties are available, the London and the Bristol. Again, these are streamlined fish with large-lobed caudal fins and enlarged dorsal fins. They are of the nacreous group and so exhibit a whole range of colours. Like the Comet, they are hardy and well suited to the outdoor pond.

Fantail: In this variety, the body is shorter than that of the common goldfish, giving an egg shape. The dorsal fin is tall and the anal and caudal fins are double.

Both metallic and nacreous types are available in a wide range of colours. The variety is hardy and suitable for tank or pond. In Japan the equivalent type is known as the 'Ryukin' and is extremely popular. One of the variants of the Fantail has telescope eyes by which is meant that the eyes are on the end of fleshy growths.

Nymph: This is a sort of Fantail in which the anal and caudal fins remain single.

Veiltail: Somewhat larger than the Fantail, the Veiltail is very popular because of its long flowing fins, which are doubled as in the fantail. The body is more spherical and metallic, and nacreous forms are available in a wide range of colours. There is also a telescope-eyed variety. Although they are reasonably hardy, these fish are better suited to the aquarium than the garden pond, because there is more risk of fin damage in the pond.

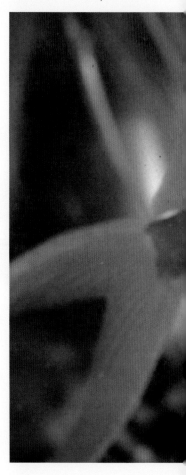

Lionhead: In Japan these fish are termed 'Ranchu' and are very highly prized. Warty, raspberry-like growths on the head (called the 'hood') are the obvious distinguishing features. Ideally, the hood should occur evenly around the head, but really good specimens are uncommon and therefore expensive. The hood means that the gill plates are inflexible, so the fish need well-aerated water so that they can breathe. The hood takes about two years to develop fully. The dorsal fin is lacking, which means the fish are less stable swimmers; there is a double caudal fin. The type is metallic.

Oranda: This variety was developed by crossing the Lionhead with the Veiltail to produce a fish showing the body features of the Veiltail with the characteristic hood of the Lionhead. Various colours are available, including the Redcap Oranda in which the body is silver while the warty head growth is red. Also popular are blue, chocolate and the red and black orandas.

Black Moors: This is an all-black Veiltail with telescope eyes. These 'telescopes' take two to three years to develop fully. This fish is of the metallic scale type. Ideally, it should be black all over but often, and especially as it ages, a bronze hue appears on the underside and the fins. This variety is very popular in Great Britain and the USA, where it is bred to a high standard for competition.

Chinese Varieties: The more exotic goldfish are usually of Chinese origin, where the unusual or the dragon-like shapes are characteristic.

Above: A Pearlscale, one of the more unusual varieties.

Below: A young Veiltail shows off its doubled, flowing fins.

BREEDING

The **Celestial** (metallic and nacreous) has telescope eyes that are turned upward - it is said so that they can gaze at emperors. The celestial's restricted vision means that it cannot search for food as successfully as other species, so you have to be careful when feeding it. It has no dorsal fin.

The **Bubble-eye** also lacks a dorsal fin, but its most distinguishing characteristic is the fluid-filled sacs below the eyes, giving the fish a most bizarre appearance. The bubble-eye will need a carefully arranged aquarium free from any sharp projections. It is not recommended for beginners.

The **Pompon** has fleshy narial septa (between the nostrils) much enlarged to form lobes known as narial bouquets. These can become very large in some specimens, and the variety may or may not have a dorsal fin. The body shape is the same as the oranda.

The **Pearlscale** is another unusual variety. The scales are silver with red and, because of their raised centres, give a pearl-like sheen. The fish's abdomen droops to give it a somewhat fat look.

There is even a tail-less goldfish, known as the **Meteor**, and many other varieties can be seen from time to time in pet and aquatic shops and the collections of experienced fanciers.

The most interesting aspect of the hobby, perhaps, is breeding your own goldfish, and anyone who wishes to exhibit his or her fish, or simply to produce stock, is strongly advised to purchase one of the more detailed books which deal with breeding in general or specifically about goldfish. In this book there is only room to look at the basic facts.

Breeding Methods

Some fish, such as the very popular Guppy, give birth to free-swimming young and so are called 'livebearers'. However, by far the greater number of species reproduce by laying eggs, and so are termed 'egglayers'. As you may already know, the goldfish is one such egglaying species. Egglayers are conveniently divided into groups according to the way in which they lay their eggs. Loosely considered, these groups include: scatterers, substrate spawners, nestbuilders, buriers and mouthbrooders.

Goldfish are egg scatterers, which means they lay eggs quite indiscriminately and show no interest in them once laid - other than to eat them! In the wild such eggs would fall into the river beds or stick to plants, rocks or any other surface, thus gaining a measure of protection from the parents, and some would be swept some distance away by the current. In the confines of an aquarium, we must protect the eggs from the parents by various means.

Fancy Pearlscale.

Sexing

Egglaying fish are difficult to sex. As the spawning period approaches, look down on the fish from above. The female's abdomen appears unevenly swollen and this swelling is due to the eggs. The male develops small white spots known as tubercles on his gill plates, head and pectoral fins.

Breeding Preparation

First, it is essential that you breed only fully fit goldfish which demonstrate excellent colour as well as body shape and finnage. It is very impractical to try to breed your fish in a community tank for two fundamental reasons: first, you will have to exert great effort to control the partners; and second, the eggs stand little chance of maturing into young fry. A single breeding tank is the absolute minimum requirement, but really you should use two or more extra tanks, so that you can separate and grade the fry as they grow.

   The breeding tank should be as large as possible and contain water at the same temperature as that in the tank in which the breeding pair were living. The temperature should be increased by 2-3°C (3-5°F) once the partners are acclimatised to it. You can divide the tank with a glass divider so that the goldfish can see each other, but otherwise introduce the male first and the female a day or so later. The only tank furnishings needed are a nylon spawning mop or such plants as Elodea, though the mop is better. Neither gravel nor other substrate is needed, but a layer of glass marbles will safeguard any eggs that fall to the tank bottom.

Spawning

The reproductive cycle starts with the fish chasing each other around the tank. Finally, the male prods the female's vent, which makes her shed her eggs. He fertilises these with his sperm,

29

Above: A Pearlscale.

Below: A Veiltail.

known as milt. The process is repeated until all the female's eggs are shed. If the pair fail to mate after being placed together, try raising the water temperature another couple of degrees. It is common practice to site a breeding tank where it will catch the early morning rays of the sun, which often stimulates breeding.

Raising The Fry

Once the eggs are shed, remove the adults, otherwise you will have very few youngsters. When they are born, the fry get their food by absorbing the yolk sac, but they will need to be fed after about three to four days. Keep your eye on the yolk sac so that you know exactly when to start feeding

Cultures of infusoria, which are collections of microscopic organisms, and

A prize winning fancy goldfish.

AILMENTS

algae, which are unicellular plants, are good starter foods. You can prepare the former by putting some chopped straw, lettuce leaves or bruised banana skin in a jar containing boiled water and then leaving it in a warm room for a few days, after which the water will be cloudy with infusoria. Add a few drops to the tank regularly each day for the fry. Alternatively, the jar can be placed higher than the tank and a plastic tube used to siphon the infusoria into the fry's tank. A clamp should be applied to control the flow so that it is reduced to a very slow, steady drip. Algae are prepared simply by placing a jar of clean water in direct sunlight: it will soon become green with algal growth.

It is possible to get infusoria tablets from your aquatic suppliers. They will also be able to supply brine shrimp eggs that you can hatch to provide live food.

Selection

As the young goldfish start to grow you must be quite ruthless in culling out any that are deformed or in other ways not up to standard. They can be placed in your adult stock tank and will soon be eaten, which is by far the most humane method of disposing of them. When the rest of the young fish reach a reasonable size, you can introduce them to your community tank.

Ailments

Your goldfish may suffer from a great range of ailments, most of which will be the result of inadequacies in their accommodation, care and maintenance. As in most aspects of life, prevention is better than cure. (Probably we all know the old saying that a stitch in time saves nine?) The following points should be regarded as essential husbandry.

Never introduce newly-acquired fish, plants, rocks or other life forms or materials into the established tank until either it has been subjected to a period of quarantine or thoroughly washed, whichever is appropriate. If this is not done, you risk introducing disease, predators, harmful chemicals or other similar and unwanted additions to the tank. For this reason, at least one small isolation tank is a sound investment.

Always try to identify the cause of a problem before trying to treat it. Treating a condition or disease wrongly is often worse than not giving any treatment at all, and many of the 'cure-all' type medications do not work well.

Make sure that you check the filtration and aeration systems regularly. The condition of the water, which should always look clear, is a most important factor to the health of your fish.

If you merely top up your tank with small amounts of water, chemical prostration might occur. Chemical prostration refers to the build-up of undesirable chemicals; while water evaporates, some chemicals do not, and eventually they will reach excessive levels. As a general rule, you should change about 50% of the water every three weeks.

Do not over-feed your fish, as uneaten food goes bad, contaminating the tank water.

Make sure that the aquarium is not located where it will be subjected to constant variations in water temperature, such as in direct sunlight or near a draughty door or window. Constantly fluctuating temperatures create stress for the animals which can lead to weakness, illness and even death.

Never attempt to accommodate more goldfish than the tank will allow. Fewer but fitter fish is a much more desirable condition than an over-crowded tank: those few extra fish can put the entire tank at risk. The recommended maximum level of stocking your aquarium is about 2.5cm (1in) of fish for each 4.5 litres of water. Remember when estimating the number of fish you can put into your tank that your fish will grow larger.

Illness in any animal is not difficult to spot; in fish, any that are not feeding normally must be watched carefully for further signs of regression. Any fish that

An oranda undergoing a colour change.

seems to be having difficulty in swimming or is swimming at an angle is obviously ailing.

Further examples of unhealthy goldfish are fish with bulging eyes compared to their normal state or which are rubbing against stones or have growths of any kind on their scales. They should be netted with care and placed in an isolation tank containing only water. In such an environment the fish are free of stress, and you can give medication appropriate to the symptoms without affecting the healthy members of your fish community.

There are a number of books on the subject of fish diseases and I recommend that you buy some so that you can recognise problems and learn the best course of action to take. Once an illness has been identified, you should take corrective steps in the main stock tank to ensure that it does not recur.

BIBLIOGRAPHY

Fancy Goldfish
Paul Paradise
RD-093
ISBN 0-79383-029-X
Clear and concise information to feeding and health concerns, care in the aquarium or pond and filtration and aeration, loaded with good full colour photos, too.
Hardcover: 175 x 260mm, 64 pages.

Goldfish Breeding and Genetics
Dr Joseph Smartt
James Bundell
TS-217
ISBN 0-7938-0090-0
For anyone seriously interested in breeding goldfish and developing new strains, this book gives the latest techniques of breeding and the latest understanding of goldfish genetics. Of value to both the amateur and the professional.
Hardcover: 178 x 254mm, 256 pages, over 200 colour photographs.

The Proper Care of Goldfish
James Geran
TW-107S
ISBN 079383158X
In simple, straightforward language, the author provides readers with all the basics required for responsible goldfish ownership. This book covers both indoor aquariums and outdoor ponds, feeding and breeding, as well as having a large section devoted to the many different goldfish varieties.
Softcover: 135mm x 210mm, 256 pages with full colour illustrations throughout.

Handbook of Fish Diseases
Dieter Untergasser
TS-123
ISBN 0-86622-703-2
Keys to recognising fish diseases and giving the right treatment are provided in easy-to-follow charts accompanied by excellent full-colour photographs. This book will save money and fishes' lives wherever it is used.
Hardcover: 276 x 214mm, 160 pages.

In this book, the sizes of the aquariums (tanks) are expressed in their capacity in litres. When tanks are sold, however, the size can be described in various different ways, such as litres or gallons; or the dimensions of the tank given in inches or centimetres. The following conversion information may be of help to you in expressing the size of your aquarium in the most convenient terms. When calculating the amount of water that your aquarium will hold, do remember that you will not be filling it completely to the top, and allow for the volume taken up by gravel, rocks and other ornaments.

- A litre is the equivalent of 1000 cubic centimetres.

- One cubic foot holds approximately 6.25 imperial gallons or 7.5 US gallons.

- 1000 cubic inches holds approximately 3.5 imperial gallons or 4.25 US gallons.